THE VALUE OF FRIENDSHIP

The Story of Jane Addams

VALUE COMMUNICATIONS, INC.
PUBLISHERS
LA JOLLA, CALIFORNIA

THE VALUE OF FRIENDSHIP

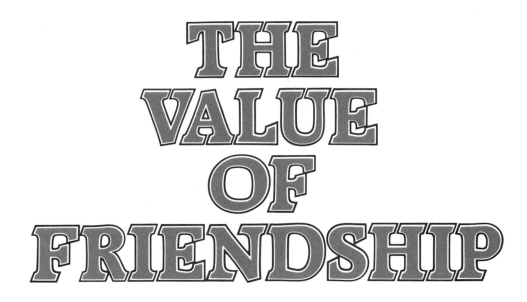

The Story of
Jane Addams

BY ANN DONEGAN JOHNSON

First Edition
Manufactured in the United States of America
For information write to: ValueTales, P.O. Box 1012
La Jolla, CA 92038

Library of Congress Cataloging in Publication Data

Johnson, Ann Donnegan.
    The value of friendship.

    (ValueTales)
    SUMMARY: Emphasizes the social changes effected by
Jane Addams as she worked to improve the lot of the poor
people who were her friends.
    1.   Addams, Jane, 1860–1935   Juvenile literature.
2.   Social workers—United States—Biography—Juvenile
literature. [1. Addams, Jane, 1860–1935.   2. Social
workers.   3. Friendship] I. Title.
HV28.A35J63   361'.92'4 [B] [92]   79-21643

ISBN 0-916392-45-7

Dedicated in memory of Tom-Tom Marsh from his friends in La Jolla

This tale is about a person who made many friends, Jane Addams. The story that follows is based on events in her life. More historical facts about Jane Addams can be found on page 63.

6

Once upon a time...
a little girl named Jane Addams lived in a lovely big house in a town called Cedarville, in Illinois.

Jane was a thin little girl, and her back wasn't quite straight. She had to carry her head tilted a bit to one side. Whenever she looked into a mirror, she sighed.

''I wish I weren't quite so homely,'' she said to herself.

Jane's mother had died when Jane was very young, so her older sisters looked after her. So did her brother. They didn't think that Jane was homely, but they did think she was too thin.

"Come on, Jane," they coaxed one morning. "Eat your breakfast. You don't want to waste away to nothing, do you?"

"Hurry with your breakfast, Jane," said her father. "I'm going into Freeport on business, and you can come with me if you finish your oatmeal."

Jane adored her handsome father, and she loved to go places with him. Quickly she ate every bit of her oatmeal, and she drank her milk. Then Mr. Addams hitched the horses to the wagon and away they went to Freeport, which was a small town not far from Cedarville.

9

Jane's father was a wealthy mill owner. He was a banker, too, and a state senator. He often had business to attend to in the towns near Cedarville. Jane had gone with him to Freeport many times.

Usually Mr. Addams drove right down the main street of the town. On this particular morning, however, he turned off onto a shabby little side street.

"We've never gone this way before," said Jane. She stared at the tumbledown houses that lined the street. Weeds grew in their tiny front yards, and torn curtains hung in their windows. Children in ragged clothes skipped out of the way as the horse and wagon passed.

"Father, what's the matter here?" whispered Jane. "Why is everything so ugly?"

"These people are very poor," said Mr. Addams. "They can't afford nice houses and pretty clothes."

Jane thought about this for a moment. Then she smiled. "When I grow up," she announced, "I'm going to build a fine big house like the one we live in. I'm going to build it here near these ugly little houses. Then the children can come and play in my yard, and I'll be their friend."

Jane went home that day to her quiet room. Her favorite doll was there. The doll stared at Jane with her glass eyes.

"Just think, Marjorie," said Jane to the doll. "There are children in Freeport who don't have anyone to care for them. They live in dirty little houses and wear ragged clothes."

The instant she said this, it seemed to her that the doll stirred. "You're wrong," the doll seemed to say. "*You* care about them, don't you?"

Jane was startled, but only for a moment. Then she laughed. "Dolls don't really talk," she said. "When I listen to you, I'm pretending, aren't I? But it's fun to pretend, Marjorie. And when I'm older, it will be fun to be friends with those children."

"Then don't forget them while you're growing up," said Marjorie. "Of course, while you're growing, the children you saw today will be growing, too. But there will always be children who need friends."

"I won't forget," said Jane.

She didn't, either—not even when there were exciting changes in her life. When she was eight, her father married again, and his new wife came to live in the lovely big house in Cedarville.

The new Mrs. Addams had two sons of her own. Harry was eighteen, and he seemed terribly grown up to Jane. But George was just Jane's age. He was an open, friendly little boy, and he liked to share things.

"Come on, Jane!" he'd call. "Let's go out to the fields and see if we can find some caterpillars."

Then he'd put on his hat with the green feather, and he'd take his toy sword in case they met any enemies. But they never needed the sword, for the creatures of the meadows were all their friends.

Jane was always so excited when she went on these trips with George that she'd forget that her back hurt or that she was too thin and probably quite homely. She followed George everywhere, and they collected caterpillars and hoptoads, tadpoles and butterflies.

"Marjorie, I'm having such fun!" Jane would say when she got home. "George is a wonderful friend!"

"He is, isn't he?" Marjorie would smile with her painted lips. "Friends are the nicest things that can happen to us."

In the evenings Jane's stepmother sat with the children in the big parlor. She had a guitar, and the family sang along with her as she played.

When she got tired of playing—or they got tired of singing—she read to the smaller children. She helped them act out plays, too, and she had parties for them and their friends.

The Addams children had never had such a good time.

But life wasn't all parties and plays for Jane. There was schoolwork, too. And there were quiet times when Jane sat alone with Marjorie and read books from her father's library.

"Such a big book for such a little girl," said her father one day. "But that's all right, Jane. I like to see you reading. In fact, I'll give you five cents for every book you finish."

"What an offer!" whispered Marjorie. "You love to read anyway. You'll make lots of money!"

Jane read on and on, and she did make quite a bit of money. More important, she read almost everything in the library, and she remembered what she read. She learned many interesting things from her father's books.

Jane grew older and taller. She wasn't so thin, and she was very bright. In fact, she was so bright that she passed the entrance examinations and was accepted as a student by Smith College in Northampton, Massachusetts.

"Isn't that wonderful?" Jane exclaimed to her father.

"It is wonderful," he agreed. "I know that not everyone is smart enough to go to Smith, and I'm proud of you. But I'm on the board of trustees for Rockford Female Seminary, Jane. People will think it strange if you don't go there. I'll have to resign my trusteeship."

18

Jane didn't want to embarrass her father or make him unhappy, so she gave up her dream of attending Smith College. She packed her trunk and went off to Rockford.

"It really isn't bad," she said when she arrived at the seminary. She was in her room pretending to talk to Marjorie, the way she had when she was a little girl. It helped to do this, especially when Jane was troubled. "If only Rockford gave a degree," she said.

Marjorie looked around the room. "It's quite cozy," she said. "The carpet is nice, and there are plenty of logs for the stove. And perhaps you can find a way to get a degree once you finish the regular courses here."

Jane had many classmates at the seminary. Before long she had a special friend, too, a girl named Ellen Gates Starr. Ellen and Jane shared their secrets, and they talked about their dreams for the future.

"So many of the girls want to go out to foreign lands and be missionaries," Jane said to Ellen. "Doesn't anyone think about the poor people here at home?"

Ellen shook her head. "It doesn't seem as if the poor people at home have many friends, does it?"

Jane looked very determined then. She remembered the shabby little houses in Freeport and the ragged children. "Someday I'm going to change all that," she said.

She studied very hard. She took math courses and science courses that frightened most of the girls, and she earned good grades. When she finished the regular three years at the seminary, she got permission to stay for an extra year and take advanced courses. Then she took her examinations and qualified for a college degree.

"You did it, Jane!" cried Marjorie. "I knew you'd find a way if you really tried!"

"Now I can study medicine," said Jane. "That will be a wonderful way to help people."

She sat down and wrote to the Women's Medical College in Philadelphia. On the basis of her outstanding work at Rockford, she was accepted. She was to enter in the fall.

But then a very sad thing happened.

In August, just as Jane was getting ready to leave for medical school, John Addams died.

Jane cried as if her heart would break. "Oh, Marjorie, what will I do?" she sobbed. "My wonderful, handsome father! He was the best friend I ever had. I miss him so much."

"Of course you do," said Marjorie. "When a friend goes away, he leaves an empty place in your heart."

Marjorie didn't tell Jane that in time there would be other friends who would help to fill the empty place. Jane would find that out for herself.

September came and Jane left for Philadelphia. Soon she was busy with her work at the medical school. There was still an empty place in her heart, but she didn't have time to think about it.

But then a trouble came that she had to think about.

Jane's old problems with her back returned. She had so much pain that she could hardly sit up. Some days she couldn't study at all.

"Jane, you can't go on this way," warned Marjorie. "You have to get help. Why don't you go to see your stepbrother?"

Jane's stepbrother, Harry Haldeman, had married Jane's sister Alice. He was now living in Iowa, where he was a very successful surgeon.

"I think I will go to him," Jane said. "I have to do something. I can't work. I can't think. I just can't stand it any longer!"

"You need an operation," said Harry after he had examined Jane. "I can fix what is hurting you, but it will take you a long time to regain your strength."

Jane agreed to the surgery, feeling it was the only way she would ever be well enough and strong enough to help others.

Even six months after the operation, Jane hadn't completely recovered. She still had to wear a heavy brace.

"Why don't you take a trip to Europe?" suggested Harry. "The experience would be wonderful for you, and you'd have time to grow really strong again. Of course you don't want to go by yourself, so Mother can go with you. Would you like that?"

Jane did not have to think about it very long before she decided that she would like it very much. "Harry is more than a stepbrother," she whispered. "He's a good friend. So is my stepmother. How lucky I am to have people who care about me."

Jane's mind went back again to the poor people no one cared about. "One day I'll do something for them," she declared.

27

As soon as Jane could get ready, she and her stepmother sailed for Europe. Jane sat on the deck of the steamship *Servia* and breathed the fresh ocean air. She felt herself growing stronger and happier by the minute.

They landed in Ireland and began touring about. Of course they saw the Blarney stone. They saw quaint cottages and great gray castles. They journeyed on to Scotland. Then they went to England, where they visited the beautiful lake region.

At last Jane and her stepmother came to London.

Do you know what they saw there?

They saw great buildings and beautiful fountains and green parks. But they saw narrow, mean streets, too, where haggard, unshaven men and thin, hungry women lived. They saw ragged, half-starved children. They even saw a market where wilted, half-rotten vegetables were auctioned off to these poor people.

Of course Jane was far too grown up now to travel about with a doll, but when she was sad or worried, she still liked to pretend that she was talking with Marjorie.

The day she saw that dreadful auction, she talked with Marjorie. "It was terrible," she told the doll. "Those people were spending their last pennies on cabbages that weren't fit to eat. Oh, Marjorie, I have to do something for the poor people. I don't know what, but I cannot let them go on like that!"

Jane spent almost two years in Europe. She traveled to many countries, and everywhere she went she saw people who needed help and friendship.

When Jane returned home, she wrote to her good friend Ellen Starr. "I feel like such a failure," she told Ellen. "For years I have thought about needy people, but I really haven't done a thing."

But then Jane remembered a place she had seen in London. It was called Toynbee Hall, and it was a building in the slums of London. Groups of educated people would come there to share their knowledge with the poor. It was called a settlement house, and it was very much like the house Jane had dreamed about when she was a child. It was a nice place set down among dirty little cottages. It was a place where poor people could come to enjoy themselves and to find friends.

"Why don't you go back to Europe?" whispered Marjorie to Jane. "Perhaps you'll see more places there that will give you good ideas about helping people."

So Jane did go back to Europe, and Ellen went with her.

When Jane and Ellen returned again to America, Jane had made up her mind. She would have a lovely big house right in the middle of a slum. She would invite the neighborhood people to her house, and she would share with them all the things she had learned at school and on her travels.

"My house will be in Chicago," she said. "You know, Ellen, in Europe the slum people at least can visit with each other. They speak the same langauge. But in Chicago there are immigrants from Italy and Germany and Poland and Russia and . . . and . . . oh, so many places. They must be very lonely."

Jane and Ellen set out to search through the city of Chicago for exactly the right house. "It has to be nice and it has to be big enough," said Jane. "If it's shabby or run-down, no one will come to it."

Now finding a large, pleasant house in the middle of a slum is never easy. Jane and Ellen searched and searched. It seemed that they saw hundreds of miles of dirty streets and thousands of broken-down old buildings.

But then at last a wonderful thing happened.

Jane was riding down Halsted Street with architect Allen Pond when she spotted a big brick house.

"Oh there it is!" she cried. "It's just what I've been looking for. Oh stop! Stop right here!"

Mr. Pond stopped and he stared. "That house?" said he. "Why, that's the old Hull mansion. It's pretty run down."

"But it's a lovely house," said Jane. "It can be fixed up. Tell me about the Hulls. Will they rent the house to me?"

Mr. Pond shrugged. "Who knows?" he said. "Charles Hull was a very wealthy man, and he built the house more than thirty years ago. When he died, the house went to his cousin, Miss Helen Culver. She owns it now, but none of the family has lived in it for a long time."

"Take me to see Miss Culver," Jane said. "I want to tell her about my plans for her house."

Miss Culver was delighted when she learned that Jane wanted to run a settlement house in the old Hull mansion.

"Halsted Street was elegant when my cousin Charles built that house," she said. "It surely isn't elegant today. But the people who live there are probably very good people. They just need a little brightness and cheer in their lives."

"Then you'll rent the house to me?" asked Jane.

"Indeed I will," replied Miss Culver, "and I'll charge you a whole dollar a year for the use of the place." She smiled. "My cousin was very fortunate," she said, "and he always wanted to give some of his money back to the city of Chicago. Perhaps this is my chance to make his wishes come true."

So Jane and Ellen happily paid the dollar in rent, and they set to work cleaning and scouring and painting and scrubbing in the old mansion. Soon Jane's other friends heard what she was doing, and they came to help, too.

"What are you going to call the place?" one of them asked.

"It already has a name," said Jane. "It's Hull House."

The people in the neighborhood gaped at the elegant ladies who came to scrub floors and clean windows and polish the door handles of the old mansion.

"What's going on here?" they said. "Surely those ladies are never going to live in *this* neighborhood!"

But then, when the house was spotless and shining, the furniture began to arrive. There were chairs and tables and sofas from Jane's own home in Cedarville. There were beautiful pictures of the towns and villages Jane had visited in Europe. There were chests of silver and crates of china and great boxes of lovely linens.

"What beautiful things!" said the neighbors. "Perhaps those ladies *are* going to live here!"

Of course that is exactly what Jane and Ellen did. They moved right into the big house, bag and baggage. At night they lit the lamps in the parlor. In the daytime they walked about in the neighborhood.

Jane did her shopping at the little grocery store down the street, and she told the grocer she hoped the neighbors would come to visit her.

As she came and went from the grocery store, she spoke to the children. She asked them if they would like to come and play at her house.

The children were polite, but they were very suspicious.

"Why would a lady like that come to live on Halsted Street?" inquired one.

"It's all very strange if you ask me," responded another.

"Oh, Ellen, they don't trust us," said Jane when she got home after one of her trips.

"It will take a little time," Ellen told her. "They aren't used to invitations from people like us. They don't understand that we just want to be friends."

Hardly had Ellen said this when there was a knock at the door.

Jane rushed to see who it was.

A dark-haired young woman stood on the steps. She had a baby in her arms, and a little girl clung to her skirts.

"The grocer said you might help me," she said. Her voice was low and soft, and she spoke with an accent. Jane knew right away that she was Italian.

44

"I have to work," said the young woman. "If I miss work, I will be fired. My friend who takes care of my children, today she is sick. I have no place to leave my baby and my little girl."

"You do have a place," said Jane. "You can leave them with us. We'll be glad to look after them. After all, we *are* neighbors, aren't we?"

Jane took the baby from the young woman, and Ellen coaxed the little girl into the parlor.

"Now off you go to work, and don't worry," said Jane.

And to herself Jane said, "Perhaps this is the beginning."

It *was* the beginning. Soon five tiny children came to Hull House each morning. There were the two Italian children and there were three others.

Jane was busy now. She hardly ever had time to talk with Marjorie as she had in the old days. But Marjorie didn't care. She was glad to see that, at last, Jane was happy.

Ellen was happy, too. She proudly showed off her five little friends when a young lady named Jenny Dow came to visit.

"They're a handful!" exclaimed Ellen. "They really keep me hopping!"

"I can see that," laughed Jenny. "Would you like for me to come and help with them?"

Jane and Ellen decided that they would like nothing better. Jenny did come, and that was the start of the Hull House kindergarten.

Soon other friends came, and there were other projects at Hull House. There were clubs where the older girls could learn sewing and cooking and dancing. There were games for the older boys, so that they wouldn't wander around the streets and get into mischief. There were plays and songs for everyone.

Hull House was beginning to be what Jane had dreamed it might be—a place where people came to visit and relax, to get to know one another, to enjoy themselves, and to learn interesting things.

As the word spread that the ladies of Hull House really were friends, the grownups began to come in the evening for coffee and cake. There was a special club room for the grownups, and the pictures there were pictures Jane had brought home from Italy. Jane's Italian neighbors sometimes felt a little homesick when they saw them, but they loved them just the same.

Before long Hull House was filled with people. The children came in the daytime. The grownups came in the evening. There was laughing and talking. People were learning things, and they were getting to know one another.

"You've done so much for them, Jane," said Marjorie.

"They've done just as much for me," Jane answered. "They've accepted me. I'm a real neighbor now, and that means a lot."

As Hull House became better known, people from wealthier areas came to help with the work there. Talented people came to share their gifts with those who weren't so fortunate.

In December, when the cold winds whistled around the corners onto Halsted Street, gifts began to arrive at Hull House.

"We're going to have a marvelous Christmas!" cried Jane. "Look at the turkeys and the potatoes. And barrels of apples! And boxes and boxes of candy! Won't the children love it!"

"I guess they will," said Ellen, "but . . . but where are the children, Jane? They haven't been coming in the afternoons lately. Do you suppose they're getting tired of the clubs and the games here?"

"Oh, I hope not!" said Jane. Then she hurried out into the neighborhood to see what was going on.

She soon learned that at Christmas and during vacations, many of the children went to work in factories nearby. They couldn't come to Hull House. They had no time.

"That's dreadful!" said Jane. "They're too young to work. But I suppose their parents really need the money."

Two days before Christmas there was a party for the girls. They all came. Jane thought they looked very tired, but she was glad to see them once again. They sang Christmas carols and they exchanged little gifts. And then it was time for supper.

Jane had planned everything carefully. There were sandwiches and cookies, and there was hot chocolate and, of course, there was plenty of candy. After all, boxes and boxes of sweets had been sent to Hull House.

But then Jenny Dow frowned and Jane looked puzzled. The girls wouldn't touch the candies. They didn't seem very happy about the cookies and the hot chocolate, either.

Finally, Jane and Ellen and Jenny learned what had happened.

The girls had been working in a candy factory nearby. For fourteen hours a day, six days a week, they had been sitting in a crowded, airless room wrapping caramels. They were sick of the sight of candy and sick of its smell.

"They probably never want to see anything sweet again as long as they live," said Marjorie to Jane.

"I'd feel exactly the same way," said Jane. "Fourteen hours a day, six days a week! That's simply terrible! It wouldn't matter whether they were wrapping candy or weaving cloth. It wouldn't matter what they were doing. Working so hard at their age could ruin their health!"

Jane and her friends began to write to the newspapers and the legislature about what had happened.

"Laws have to be passed against this sort of thing," said Jane. "Children have to be protected."

"The factory owners aren't going to like this," warned Marjorie. "They're going to fight you. You know they don't have to pay children as much as they do grownups."

The factory owners didn't like it, and they did fight. But in time a child labor law was passed—mainly as a result of the work done by residents at Hull House. It stated that children under fourteen could not work and children under sixteen could work only for eight hours a day.

Jane was delighted to know that she could make things happen, important things like child labor laws.

"Now that that's taken care of, maybe I can do something about the garbage in the streets," said Jane. "It's unhealthy and it smells terrible! The garbage men simply aren't doing their job."

Now perhaps most ladies at that time would not have wanted to have anything to do with garbage, but Jane went right out and got a job as garbage inspector for her area.

Every morning Jane started off bright and early. She followed the garbage carts up one street and down another. She watched the way the men picked up the garbage.

"You there!" she shouted at one man. "Your cart is too full. You're going to spill the garbage into the street before you ever get to the dump."

"It's not right for a woman to be a garbage inspector," grumbled the man.

Jane paid no attention to the grumbling, and she insisted that the city send out more garbage wagons. Before long the conditions in the slums began to get better. The streets were cleaner, and there wasn't nearly as much smell.

After that, Jane never stopped fighting. She worked all her life for the poor people who were her friends.

It was because of Jane that the first playground was built in Chicago. It was because of Jane that more schools were built in the city. And it was partly because of her that women got the right to vote.

Jane had very advanced ideas for the time. She even tried to get people to organize country camps so that city children could have a vacation in the open fields and the forests.

In time, Jane became famous. People in other cities copied her ideas and began to build settlement houses in poor areas. Senators and prime ministers and princes came to visit Hull House and to talk with Jane. Once even the President of the United States came.

No doubt Jane found it pleasant to be famous and admired and sought after, but that wasn't what really made her happy. What really made her happy was that she had proved herself a friend to the people around her, and they had returned her friendship.

You may not need a settlement house in your city. You may not want to change the laws in your state. But you might decide that you want to think a bit about friendship. If you do, you'll probably decide that, without friends, we are alone. When we have friends, we can do more. We can learn about new ideas. We can share what we have, and we can grow while we're doing it.

You may decide that it's important to be able to give friendship, and it's also important to be able to accept it . . .

Just like our good friend Jane Addams.

62

The End

Jane Addams was born in Cedarville, Illinois, on September 6, 1860. She was the youngest of five children of John Addams, a wealthy mill owner who was also a state senator and a banker.

Jane's mother died when Jane was still a baby, so the sensitive little girl was looked after by her older sisters and her brother. She suffered great mental anguish because a curvature of the spine caused her head to droop to one side, and she felt this slight deformity made her very ugly.

Jane was seven when she first became aware of poverty. On a shabby street in a town near Cedarville, she saw ragged children and dirty little houses. She announced that she wanted to build a big house among the smaller ones so that the poor children would have a place to come and play.

When Jane was eight, her father married a widow named Anna Haldeman. The new Mrs. Addams had two sons: Harry, who was eighteen, and George, who was just six months younger than Jane. George was an adventurous, outgoing boy who helped expand shy little Jane's horizons.

In 1881, Jane graduated from Rockford Female Seminary at Rockford, Illinois. Most young ladies who graduated from that school received only a certificate; however, Jane insisted upon remaining at Rockford for an extra year and taking advanced courses and examinations so that she could qualify a full college degree. She promptly enrolled in the Philadelphia Women's College, intending to become a physician.

Almost immediately, Jane had to abandon her hopes for a career in medicine. During her first year in Philadelphia, the trouble she had always had with her back became serious enough to require surgery. While she was recovering, she traveled in Europe. She saw the deplorable living conditions of the poor people in the slums there, and she was touched and troubled.

On a second trip to Europe with Ellen Starr, a schoolmate from Rockford, Jane visited the London settlement house called Toynbee Hall. She saw educated people who had come to help the poor and live among them as neighbors. Impressed with this concept, Jane and Ellen returned to the United States. They searched through the slums of Chicago until they found the Hull mansion, abandoned and in disrepair, at

JANE ADDAMS
1860–1935

334 South Halsted Street. Deciding that this would make an ideal settlement house, they rented the place, cleaned it, furnished it, and moved in to live as neighbors to the people in the surrounding area.

Soon Jane and Ellen were caring for the children of working mothers at Hull House. Women came from more affluent areas to help teach classes in sewing and cooking and dressmaking. Older boys and girls had clubs at the mansion, and senior residents of the neighborhood came to attend "old settlers' parties."

Jane soon found that there were needs in the slums which a settlement house alone could not meet. Children were working in sweat shops, so Jane fought for child labor laws. People were being injured in factories, so she urged Congress to pass laws governing safety conditions. She campaigned for adult education, day nurseries, better housing, and women's suffrage. Her fame and influence spread. She became the recipient of the first honorary degree ever bestowed on a woman by Yale University. President Theodore Roosevelt called her "America's most useful citizen."

In 1931, Jane was awarded the Nobel Peace Prize. She died four years later, on May 21, 1935. She was almost 75, and still a resident of Hull House, and a friend to her neighbors on Halsted Street.

The ValueTale Series